LAW ON INTELLECTUAL PROPERTY

Essential Legal Terms Explained You Need To Know About Trademarks, Copyrights, Patents, and Trade Secrets!

DR. PETER JOHNSON

ISBN: 9781798993774

Legal & disclaimer

The information contained in this book and its contents is not designed to replace or take the place of any form of medical or professional advice; and is not meant to replace the need for independent medical, financial, legal or other professional advice or services, as may be required. The content and information in this book have been provided for educational and entertainment purposes only.

The content and information contained in this book have been compiled from sources deemed reliable, and it is accurate to the best of the author's knowledge, information, and belief. However, the author cannot guarantee its accuracy and validity and cannot be held liable for any errors and/or omissions. Further, changes are periodically made to this book as and when needed. Where appropriate and/or necessary, you must consult a professional (including but not limited to your doctor, attorney, financial advisor or such other professional advisor) before using any of the suggested remedies, techniques, or information in this book.

Upon using the contents and information contained in this book, you agree to hold harmless the author from and against any damages, costs, and expenses, including any legal fees potentially resulting from the application of any of the information provided by this book. This disclaimer applies to any loss, damages or injury caused by the use and application, whether directly or indirectly, of any advice or information presented, whether for breach of contract, tort, negligence, personal injury, criminal intent, or under any other cause of action.

You agree to accept all risks of using the information presented inside this book.

You agree that by continuing to read this book, where appropriate and/or necessary, you shall consult a professional (including but not limited to your doctor, attorney, or financial advisor or such other advisor as needed) before using any of the suggested remedies, techniques, or information in this book.

Table of Contents

Acts Of Unfair Competition

Obligation To Use Inventions And Marks

General Provisions On Assignment Of Industrial Property Rights

Restrictions On Assignment Of Industrial Property Rights

Contents Of Industrial Property Right Assignment Contracts

Licensing Of Industrial Property Rights

Restrictions On Licensing Of Industrial Property Objects

Types Of Industrial Property Object Licence Contracts

Contents Of Industrial Property Object Licence Contracts

Industrial Property Representation Services

Scope Of Rights Of Industrial Property Representatives

Responsibilities Of Industrial Property Representatives

Conditions Applicable To Industrial Property Representation Service Business

Conditions Applicable To Industrial Property Representation Service Practices

Organizations And Individuals Whose Rights To Plant Varieties Are Eligible For Protection

Distinctness Of A Plant Variety

Uniformity Of A Plant Variety

Stability Of A Plant Variety

Licensing Of Plant Varieties

Introduction

Thank you and congratulate you for downloading the book *"LAW ON INTELLECTUAL PROPERTY: Essential Legal Terms Explained You Need To Know About Trademarks, Copyrights, Patents, and Trade Secrets"*

With a clear, concise, and engaging writing style, Dr. Peter Johnson will help you with a practical understanding of intellectual property law topics about *Trademarks, Copyrights, Patents, and Trade Secrets*; provide you a road map to navigating intellectual property rules and help you build a foundation for understanding the overall picture and much much more. This book delivers extensive coverage of every aspect of the law and details the duties a paralegal is expected to perform when working within intellectual property law. High-level, comprehensive coverage is combined with cutting-edge developments and foundational concepts.

As the author of the book, I promise this book will be an invaluable source of legal reference for professionals, international lawyers, law students, business professionals and anyone else who want to improve their use of legal terminology, succinct clarification of legal terms and have a better understanding of law on intellectual property. All legal terms and phrases are well written and explained clearly in plain English.

Thank you again for purchasing this book, and I hope you enjoy it.

Let's get started!

GENERAL PROVISIONS

This Law regulates copyright, copyright related rights, industrial property rights and rights to plant varieties; and the protection of such rights.

SUBJECT MATTER OF INTELLECTUAL PROPERTY RIGHTS

1. The subject matter of copyright shall comprise literary, artistic and scientific works; the subject matter of copyright related rights shall comprise performances, audio and visual fixation, broadcasts and satellite signals carrying coded programmes.

2. The subject matter of industrial property rights shall comprise inventions, industrial designs, designs of semi-conducting closed circuits, trade secrets, marks, trade names and geographical indications.

3. The subject matter of rights to plant varieties shall comprise plant varieties and reproductive materials.

INTERPRETATION OF TERMS

1. *Intellectual property rights* means rights of an organization or individual to intellectual assets comprising copyright and copyright related rights, industrial property rights and rights to plant varieties.

2. *Copyright* means rights of an organization or individual to works which such organization or individual created or owns.

3. *Copyright related rights* (hereinafter referred to as related rights) means rights of an organization or individual to performances, audio and visual fixation, and broadcasts and satellite signals carrying coded programmes.

4. *Industrial property rights* means rights of an organization or individual to inventions, industrial designs, designs of semi-conducting closed circuits, trade secrets, marks, trade names and geographical indications which such organization or individual created or owns, and the right to prevent unfair competition.

5. *Rights to plant varieties* means rights of an organization or individual to new plant varieties which such organization or individual has selected and created, discovered and developed, or which they own.

6. *Intellectual property right holder* means an owner of intellectual property rights or an organization or individual to whom intellectual property rights are assigned by the owner.

7. *Work* means a creation of the mind in the literary, artistic or scientific sector, expressed in any mode or form.

8. *Derivative work* means a work translated from one language into another; or an adapted, modified, transformed, compiled, annotated or selected work.

9. *Published work, audio and visual fixation* means a work or audio and visual fixation which has been published with the permission of the copyright holder or related right holder in order to distribute it to the public in a reasonable amount of copies.

10. *Reproduction* means the making of one or more copies of a work, audio and visual fixation by whatever mode or in whatever form, including permanent or provisional backup of the work in electronic form.

11. *Broadcasting* means the transmission of sound or image or both sound and image of a work, performance, audio and visual fixation or broadcast to the public by wireless or landline means including satellite transmission, in such a way that the public may access such work from any place and time the public selects.

12. *Invention* means a technical solution in the form of a product or process which is intended to solve a problem by application of natural laws.

13. *Industrial design* means the outward appearance of a product embodied in three-dimensional configuration, lines, colours or a combination of such elements.

14. *Semiconductor integrated circuit* means a product in its intermediate or final form in which the elements, at least one of which is an active element, and some or all of the interconnections, are integrally formed in or on a piece of semiconductor material and which is intended to

perform an electronic function. Integrated circuit is synonymous with IC, chip and micro-electronic circuit.

15. *Design of semi-conducting closed circuits* (hereinafter referred to as layout design) means a three-dimensional disposition of circuit elements and their interconnections in a semi-conducting closed circuit.

16. *Mark* means any sign used to distinguish goods or services of different organizations or individuals.

17. *Collective mark* means a mark used to distinguish goods or services of members of an organization which is the owner of such mark from marks of non-members of such organization.

18. *Certification mark* means a mark which is authorized by its owner to be used by another organization or individual on the latter's goods or services in order to certify the origin, raw materials, materials, mode of manufacture of goods or manner of provision of services, and the quality, accuracy, safety or other characteristic of goods or services bearing such mark.

19. *Integrated marks* means identical or similar marks registered by the same entity and intended for use on products or services which are of the same, similar or interrelated type.

20. *Well known mark* means a mark widely known by consumers throughout the territory of Vietnam.

21. *Trade name* means the designation of an organization or individual used in business activities in order to distinguish the business entity bearing such trade name from other business entities in the same business sector and area.

Business area as stipulated in this clause means the geographical area in which a business entity has its partners, customers or reputation.

22. *Geographical indication* means the sign used to identify a product as originating from a specific region, locality, territory or country.

23. *Trade secret* means information obtained from activities of financial or intellectual investment, which has not yet been disclosed and which is able to be used in business.

24. *Plant variety* means a plant grouping within a single botanical taxon of the lowest known rank, which is morphologically uniform and suitable for being propagated unchanged, and can be defined by the expression of phenotypes resulting from a genotype or a combination of given genotypes, and distinguished from any other plant grouping by the expression of at least one inheritable phenotype.

25. *Protection title* means a document granted by the competent State body to an organization or individual in order to establish industrial property rights to an invention, industrial design, layout design, mark or geographical indication; or in order to establish rights to a plant variety.

GROUNDS FOR THE GENERATION AND ESTABLISHMENT OF INTELLECTUAL PROPERTY RIGHTS

1. Copyright shall arise at the moment a work is created and fixed in a certain material form, irrespective of its content, quality, form, mode and language and irrespective of whether or not such work has been published or registered.

2. Related rights shall arise at the moment a performance, audio and visual fixation, broadcast or satellite signal carrying coded programmes is fixed or displayed without causing loss or damage to copyright.

POLICIES OF THE STATE ON INTELLECTUAL PROPERTY

1. To recognize and protect intellectual property rights of organizations and individuals on the basis of harmonizing the interests of intellectual property right holders and the public interest; not to protect intellectual property objects which are contrary to social ethics and public order or which harm national defence and security.

2. To encourage and promote activities of creation and utilization of intellectual assets aimed at contributing to socio-economic development and improving the people's material and spiritual life.

3. To provide financial support for the receipt and use of transferred intellectual property rights servicing the public interest; to encourage organizations and individuals to provide financial aid for creative activities and for the protection of intellectual property rights.

4. To prioritize investment in training and fostering senior officials, public servants and other relevant subjects engaged in the work of protecting intellectual property rights and to prioritize research into and application of science and techniques for the protection of intellectual property rights.

RIGHT AND RESPONSIBILITY OF ORGANIZATIONS AND INDIVIDUALS IN THE PROTECTION OF INTELLECTUAL PROPERTY RIGHTS

Organizations and individuals shall have the right to themselves take measures permitted by law to protect their intellectual property rights, and shall be obliged to respect the intellectual property rights of other organizations and individuals in accordance with the provisions of Law on intellectual property and other relevant laws.

TYPES OF WORKS WHICH ARE PROTECTED BY COPYRIGHT

Literary, artistic and scientific works which are protected by copyright comprise:

(a) Literary works, scientific works, textbooks, teaching courses and other works expressed in written language or other characters;

(b) Lectures, addresses and other speeches;

(c) Press works;

(d) Musical works;

(dd) Stage works;

(e) Cinematographic works and works created by a process analogous to cinematography (hereinafter all referred to as cinematographic works);

(g) Plastic art works and applied art works;

(h) Photographic works;

(i) Architectural works;

(k) Sketches, plans, maps and drawings related to topography or scientific works;

(l) Folklore and folk-art works;

(m) Computer programs and data collections.

COPYRIGHT

Copyright in works regulated in Law on intellectual property shall comprise moral rights and economic rights.

MORAL RIGHTS

Moral rights [of authors] shall comprise the following rights:

1. To give titles to their works.

2. To attach their real names or pseudonyms to their works; to have their real names or pseudonyms acknowledged when their works are published or used.

3. To publish their works or to authorize other persons to publish their works.

4. To protect the integrity of their works; and to forbid other persons to modify, edit or distort their works in whatever form, causing harm to the honour and reputation of the author.

ECONOMIC RIGHTS

Economic rights [of authors] shall comprise the following rights:

(a) To make derivative works;

(b) To display their works to the public;

(c) To reproduce their works;

(d) To distribute or import the original or copies of their works;

(dd) To communicate their works to the public by wireless or landline means, electronic information networks or other technical means;

(e) To lease the original or copies of cinematographic works and computer programs.

COPYRIGHT IN COMPUTER PROGRAMS AND DATA COLLECTIONS

1. Computer program means a set of instructions expressed in the form of commands, codes, diagrams and other forms which, when incorporated in a device readable by a computer, are capable of enabling such computer to perform a job or achieve a specific result.

Computer programs shall be protected the same as literary works, irrespective of whether the computer programs are expressed in the form of source codes or machine codes.

2. Data collection means a set of data selected or arranged in a creative way and expressed in electronic or other forms.

Copyright protection of data collections shall not extend to protection of the data itself, and must not be prejudicial to copyright in the data itself.

COPYRIGHT IN FOLKLORE AND FOLK-ART WORKS

1. Folklore and folk-art work means a collective creation based on the traditions of a community or individuals reflecting the ambitions of such community and expressed in a form appropriate to the cultural and social characteristics, standards and values of such community which have been handed down by imitation or other modes. Folklore and folk-art works shall comprise:

(a) Folk tales, lyrics and riddles;

(b) Folk songs and melodies;

(c) Folk dances, plays, rites and games;

(d) Folk art products including graphics, paintings, sculpture, musical instruments, architectural models and other artistic expressions in any material form.

2. Organizations and individuals using folklore and folk-art works must cite the origins of the folklore and folk-art works, and must ensure that the authentic value of such folklore and folk art works is preserved.

CASES WHEN PUBLISHED WORKS MAY BE USED WITHOUT HAVING TO SEEK PERMISSION OR PAY ROYALTIES OR REMUNERATION

1. Published works may be used without having to seek permission or pay royalties or remuneration in the following cases:

(a) Making one copy of the work of an author for scientific research or teaching purposes;

(b) Reasonable quoting from a work in order to comment on or illustrate one's own works, without misrepresenting the author's views;

(c) Quoting from a work in order to write an article published in a newspaper or periodical, in a radio or television broadcast or in a documentary, without misrepresenting the author's views;

(d) Quoting from a work in school or university for lecturing purposes without misrepresenting the author's views and not for commercial purposes;

(dd) Copying of a work by a library for archival and research purposes;

(e) Performing a stage work or other art work in mass cultural, communication or mobilization activities without collecting fees in any form;

(g) Audio-visual recording of a performance in order to report current events or for teaching purposes;

(h) Photographing or televising plastic art; or an architectural, photographic, or applied art work displayed at a public place in order to present images of such work;

(i) Transcribing a work into braille or into characters of other languages for the blind;

(k) Importing copies of another's work for personal use.

CASES WHEN PUBLISHED WORKS MAY BE USED WITHOUT HAVING TO SEEK PERMISSION BUT ROYALTIES OR REMUNERATION MUST BE PAID

A broadcasting organization which uses a published work to make a broadcast which is sponsored, contains an advertisement or which collects fees in any form shall not be required to seek permission but must pay royalties or remuneration to the copyright holder in accordance with regulations of the Government.

RIGHTS OF PERFORMERS

1. Performers who are also the investors shall have the moral rights and economic rights to their performances. Where performers are not also the investors, the performers shall have the moral rights and the investors shall have the economic rights to performances.

2. Moral rights shall comprise the following rights:

(a) To have the name acknowledged when performing, when distributing audio and visual fixation or when broadcasting performances;

(b) To protect the integrity of the imagery of the performance, and to prevent others from modifying, editing or distorting the work in any way prejudicial to the honour and reputation of the performer.

3. Economic rights shall include the exclusive right to exercise or to authorize others to exercise the following rights:

(a) To formulate a live performance on audio and visual fixation;

(b) To directly or indirectly reproduce a performance which has been formulated on audio and visual fixation;

(c) To broadcast or to communicate to the public in other ways an unformulated performance so that it may be accessed by the public, except where such performance is intended to be broadcast;

(d) To distribute to the public an original performance and copies thereof by sale, rental or distribution by whatever technical means which are accessible by the public.

RIGHTS OF PRODUCERS OF AUDIO AND VISUAL FIXATION

1. Producers of audio and visual fixation shall have the exclusive right to exercise, or to authorize others to exercise, the following rights:

(a) To directly or indirectly copy their audio and visual fixation;

(b) To distribute to the public their original audio and visual fixation and copies thereof by sale, rent or distribution by whatever technical means which are accessible by the public.

2. Producers of audio and visual fixation shall be entitled to material benefits when such recording is distributed to the public.

RIGHTS OF BROADCASTING ORGANIZATIONS

1. Broadcasting organizations shall have the exclusive right to exercise, or to authorize others to exercise, the following rights:

(a) To broadcast or re-broadcast their broadcasts;

(b) To distribute their broadcasts to the public;

(c) To formulate [into a fixed form] their broadcasts;

(d) To reproduce formulated broadcasts.

2. Broadcasting organizations shall be entitled to material benefits when their broadcasts are recorded and distributed to the public.

CASES WHEN RELATED RIGHTS MAY BE EXERCISED WITHOUT HAVING TO SEEK PERMISSION OR PAY ROYALTIES OR REMUNERATION

Related rights may be exercised without having to seek permission or pay royalties or remuneration in the following cases:

(a) Making one copy of a work for personal scientific research purposes;

(b) Making one copy of a work for teaching purposes, except for performances, audio and visual fixation or broadcasts which have been published for teaching purposes;

(c) Reasonable quoting from a work in order to provide information;

(d) Making of provisional copies of a work by a broadcasting organization for broadcasting purposes when such organization has the broadcasting right.

CASES WHEN RELATED RIGHTS MAY BE EXERCISED WITHOUT HAVING TO SEEK PERMISSION BUT WHEN ROYALTIES OR REMUNERATION MUST BE PAID

Organizations and individuals who exercise related rights in the following cases shall not be required to seek permission but must pay agreed royalties or remuneration to performers, producers of audio and visual fixation, or to broadcasting organizations:

(a) They directly or indirectly use published audio and visual fixation for commercial purposes in making broadcasts which are sponsored, contain advertisements or which collect fees in any form;

(b) They use published audio and visual fixation in business or commercial activities.

CONDUCT CONSTITUTING INFRINGEMENT OF RELATED RIGHTS

1. Appropriating the rights of a performer, producer of audio and visual fixation, or of a broadcasting organization.

2. Impersonating a performer, producer of audio and visual fixation, or a broadcasting organization.

3. Publishing, producing and distributing a formulated performance, audio and visual fixation or a broadcast without permission from the performer, producer of the audio and visual fixation or from the broadcasting organization.

4. Modifying, editing or distorting a performance in any way which prejudices the honour and reputation of the performer.

5. Copying or reciting from a formulated performance, audio and visual fixation or a broadcast without permission from the performer, producer of the audio and visual fixation or from the broadcasting organization.

6. Deliberately deleting or modifying electronic information regarding management of rights without permission from the related right holder.

7. Deliberately destroying or de-activating the technical solutions applied by the related right holder to protect his or her rights.

8. Publishing, distributing or importing for public distribution performances, copies of a fixed performance or audio and visual fixation knowing, or having grounds to know, that electronic information regarding management of rights has been deleted or modified without permission from the related right holder.

9. Manufacturing, assembling, transforming, distributing, importing, exporting, selling or leasing out equipment knowing, or having grounds to know, that such equipment helps to illegally decode satellite signals carrying coded programmes.

10. Deliberately receiving or relaying satellite signals carrying coded programmes without permission from the legal distributor.

COPYRIGHT HOLDERS BEING AUTHORS

Authors who use their own time, finance and material or technical facilities to create works shall have the moral rights.

COPYRIGHT HOLDERS BEING CO-AUTHORS

1. Co-authors who use their time, finance and material or technical facilities to jointly create works shall share the rights to such works.

2. A co-author who has jointly created a work, a separate part of which is detachable for independent use without prejudice to the parts of the work of the other co- authors, shall have the rights to such separate part.

COPYRIGHT HOLDERS BEING THE STATE

The State shall be the holder of copyright in the following works:

(a) Anonymous works;

(b) Works for which the term of protection has not expired but the copyright holder died without leaving an heir or the heir renounced the inheritance or was deprived of the right to inherit;

(c) Works for which the ownership right was assigned to the State by the copyright holder.

RELATED RIGHT HOLDERS

1. Organizations and individuals who use their time and make a financial investment in or use their material and technical facilities to give a performance shall be the owners of such performance unless otherwise agreed with the parties concerned.

2. Organizations and individuals who use their time and make a financial investment in or use their material and technical facilities to produce audio and visual fixation shall be the owners of such audio and visual fixation unless otherwise agreed with the parties concerned.

3. Broadcasting organizations shall be the owners of their broadcasts unless otherwise agreed with the parties concerned.

ASSIGNMENT OF COPYRIGHT AND RELATED RIGHTS

1. Assignment of copyright and related rights means the transfer by copyright holders or related right holders of the ownership of the rights to other organizations and individuals pursuant to a contract or in accordance with a relevant provision of law.

2. Authors and performers shall not be permitted to assign the moral rights.

3. Where a work, performance, audio and visual fixation or broadcast is under joint ownership, the assignment thereof must be agreed upon by all co-owners. In a case of joint ownership of a work, performance, audio and visual fixation or broadcast which is composed of separate parts detachable for independent use, copyright holders or related right holders may assign their copyright or related rights in their separate parts to other organizations or individuals.

CONTRACTS FOR THE ASSIGNMENT OF COPYRIGHT OR RELATED RIGHTS

A contract for the assignment of copyright or related rights must be made in writing and include the following principal contents:

(a) Names and addresses of the assignor and the assignee;

(b) Grounds for the assignment;

(c) Price and method of payment;

(d) Rights and obligations of the parties;

(dd) Liability for contractual breach.

LICENSING OF COPYRIGHT AND RELATED RIGHTS

1. Licensing of copyright and related rights means the grant of permission by the copyright holder or related right holder for another organization or individual to use for a definite term one, several or all of the rights stipulated in Law on intellectual property.

2. Authors shall not be permitted to license the moral rights except for the right of publication. Performers shall not be permitted to license the moral rights.

3. Where a work, performance, audio and visual fixation or broadcast is under joint ownership, the licensing of copyright or related rights therein must be agreed upon by all co-owners. In a case of joint ownership of a work, performance, audio and visual fixation or broadcast which is composed of separate parts detachable for independent use, copyright holders or related right holders may license their copyright or related rights in their separate parts to other organizations or individuals.

4. Any organization or individual to whom copyright or related rights are licensed shall be permitted to license other organizations and individuals after obtaining permission from the copyright holder or related right holder.

CONTRACTS FOR THE LICENSING OF COPYRIGHT OR RELATED RIGHTS

A contract for the licensing of copyright or related rights must be made in writing and include the following principal contents:

(a) Full names and addresses of the licensor and the licensee;

(b) Grounds for the licence;

(c) Scope of the licence;

(d) Price and method of payment;

(dd) Rights and obligations of the parties;

(e) Liability for contractual breach.

REGISTRATION OF COPYRIGHT AND RELATED RIGHTS

1. Registration of copyright and related rights means the filing of an application with a file enclosed (hereinafter referred to as application) by an author, copyright holder or related rights holder with the competent State body in order to record information on the author, the work, the copyright holder and the related rights holder.

2. The filing of an application for grant of a certificate of registered copyright or a certificate of registered related rights shall not be a compulsory pre-requisite for entitlement to copyright or related rights in accordance with the provisions of Law on intellectual property.

3. Organizations and individuals who are granted certificates of registered copyright or certificates of registered related rights shall not bear the burden of proving such copyright or related rights in a dispute, unless contrary proof is tendered.

APPLICATIONS FOR REGISTRATION OF COPYRIGHT OR RELATED RIGHTS

1. Authors, copyright holders and related rights holders may directly file, or may authorize other organizations or individuals to file, applications for registration of copyright or related rights.

2. An application for registration of copyright or related rights shall comprise:

(a) A declaration for registration of copyright or related rights.

A declaration must be signed by the author, copyright holder, related rights holder or person authorized to file the application; and must include complete information on the applicant, author, copyright holder or related rights holder; the summarized content of the work, performance, audio and visual fixation or broadcast; the name of the author, and the title of the work used to make the derivative work if the work to be registered is a derivative work; the date, place and form of publication; and an undertaking accepting liability for the information set out in the application.

(b) Two copies of the work the subject of the application for copyright registration, or two copies of the formulated object the subject of the application for related rights registration;

(c) A letter of authorization where the applicant is an authorized person;

(d) Documents proving the right to file the application where the applicant acquires such right by way of inheritance, succession or assignment;

(dd) Written consent of the co-authors in the case of a work under joint authorship;

(e) Written consent of the co-owners if the copyright or related rights are jointly owned.

ORGANIZATIONS ACTING AS COLLECTIVE REPRESENTATIVES OF COPYRIGHT OR RELATED RIGHTS

1. An organization acting as the collective representative of copyright or related rights means a non-profit making organization established pursuant to an agreement between authors, copyright holders or related right holders and operating pursuant to the law on protection of copyright and related rights.

2. An organization acting as the collective representative of copyright or related rights may conduct the following activities pursuant to authorization from authors, copyright holders or related right holders:

(a) Manage copyright or related rights; conduct negotiations for licensing; and collect and distribute royalties, remuneration and other material benefits from the permitted exercise of authorized rights;

(b) Protect the legitimate rights and interests of its members; organize a conciliation if a dispute arises.

3. An organization acting as the collective representative of copyright or related rights shall have the following rights and duties:

(a) To encourage creative and other social activities;

(b) To co-operate with counterparts in international and national organizations on the protection of copyright and related rights;

(c) To make periodic and one-off reports to competent State bodies on its collective representative activities;

(d) Other rights and duties stipulated by law.

CONDITIONS FOR INVENTIONS TO BE ELIGIBLE FOR PROTECTION

1. An invention shall be eligible for protection in the form of the grant of an invention patent when it satisfies the following conditions:

(a) It is novel;

(b) It is of an inventive nature;

(c) It is susceptible of industrial application.

2. Unless an invention is common knowledge, it shall be protected in the form of the grant of a utility solution patent when it satisfies the following conditions:

(a) It is novel;

(b) It is susceptible of industrial application.

OBJECTS INELIGIBLE FOR PROTECTION AS INVENTIONS

The following objects shall be ineligible for protection as inventions:

1. Scientific discoveries or theories, mathematical methods.

2. Schemes, plans, rules and methods for performing mental acts, training domestic animals, playing games and doing business; computer programs.

3. Presentations of information.

4. Solutions of aesthetic characteristics only.

5. Plant varieties, animal breeds.

7. Processes of plant or animal production which are principally of a biological nature, other than microbiological processes.

8. Human and animal disease prevention methods, diagnostic and treatment methods.

NOVELTY OF INVENTIONS

1. An invention shall be deemed novel if it has not yet been publicly disclosed by use or by means of a written description or any other form before the filing date or the priority date, as applicable, of the invention registration application.

2. An invention shall be deemed not yet publicly disclosed if it is known to only a limited number of persons who are obliged to keep it secret.

CONDITIONS FOR INDUSTRIAL DESIGNS TO BE ELIGIBLE FOR PROTECTION

An industrial design shall be eligible for protection when it satisfies the following conditions:

(a) It is novel;

(b) It is of a creative nature;

(c) It is susceptible of industrial application.

OBJECTS INELIGIBLE FOR PROTECTION AS INDUSTRIAL DESIGNS

The following items shall be ineligible for protection as industrial designs:

1. Outward appearance of a product which is necessarily due to the technical features of the product.

2. Outward appearance of civil or industrial construction works.

3. Shape of a product which is invisible during the use of the product.

CONDITIONS FOR LAYOUT DESIGNS TO BE ELIGIBLE FOR PROTECTION

A layout design shall be eligible for protection when it satisfies the following conditions:

1. It is original.
2. It is commercially novel.

OBJECTS INELIGIBLE FOR PROTECTION AS LAYOUT DESIGNS

The following items shall be ineligible for protection as layout designs:

1. Principles, processes, systems and methods operated by semiconductor integrated circuits.
2. Information or software contained in semiconductor integrated circuits.

ORIGINALITY OF LAYOUT DESIGNS

A layout design shall be deemed to be original if it satisfies the following conditions:

(a) It is the result of its author's creative labour;

(b) It was not widely known among creators of layout designs or manufacturers of semi-conducting closed circuits at the time of its creation.

CONDITIONS FOR MARKS TO BE ELIGIBLE FOR PROTECTION

A mark shall be eligible for protection when it satisfies the following conditions:

1. It is a visible sign in the form of letters, words, drawings or images including holograms, or a combination thereof, represented in one or more colours.

2. It is capable of distinguishing goods or services of the mark owner from those of other subjects.

CRITERIA FOR EVALUATION OF WHETHER OR NOT A MARK IS WELL KNOWN

The following criteria shall be taken into account when considering whether or not a mark is well known:

1. The number of relevant consumers who were aware of the mark by purchase or use of goods or services bearing the mark, or from advertising.

2. The territorial area in which goods or services bearing the mark are circulated.

3. Turnover of the sale of goods or provision of services bearing the mark or the quantity of goods sold or services provided.

4. Duration of continuous use of the mark.

5. Wide reputation of goods or services bearing the mark.

6. Number of countries protecting the mark.

7. Number of countries recognizing the mark as a well-known mark.

8. Assignment price, licensing price, or investment capital contribution value of the mark.

CONDITIONS FOR TRADE NAMES TO BE ELIGIBLE FOR PROTECTION

A trade name shall be protected when it is capable of distinguishing the business entity bearing it from other business entities operating in the same business sector and locality.

DISTINCTIVENESS OF TRADE NAMES

A trade name shall be deemed to be distinctive when it satisfies the following conditions:

1. It consists of a proper name, except where the proper name was widely known by use.

2. It is not identical with or confusingly similar to a trade name which was used earlier by another person in the same business sector and locality.

3. It is not identical with or confusingly similar to another person's mark or a geographical indication which was protected before the date of use of such trade name.

CONDITIONS FOR TRADE SECRETS TO BE ELIGIBLE FOR PROTECTION

A trade secret shall be eligible for protection when it satisfies the following conditions:

1. It is neither common knowledge nor easily obtainable.

2. When used in business activities, the trade secret will create for its holder advantages over those who do not hold or use it.

3. The owner of the trade secret maintains its secrecy by necessary means so that the secret will not be disclosed nor be easily accessible

OBJECTS INELIGIBLE FOR PROTECTION AS TRADE SECRETS

The following confidential information shall be ineligible for protection as trade secrets:

1. Personal identification secrets.
2. State management secrets.
3. National defence and security secrets.
4. Other confidential information unrelated to business.

PROTECTION TITLES

1. A protection title shall recognize the owner of the invention, industrial design, layout design or mark (hereinafter all referred to as protection title owners); the author of the invention, industrial design or layout design; and the subject matter, scope and term of protection.

2. A protection title of a geographical indication shall record the organization managing such geographical indication, the organization or individual having the right to use such geographical indication, the protected geographical indication, the particular characteristics of products bearing such geographical indication, and the particular characteristics of geographical conditions and geographical areas bearing such geographical indication.

3. Protections title shall include an invention patent, utility solution patent, industrial design patent, certificate of registered design of semi-conducting closed circuits, certificate of registered mark and certificate of registered geographical indication.

TERMINATION OF VALIDITY OF PROTECTION TITLES

The validity of a protection title shall be terminated in the following cases:

(a) The owner fails to pay the stipulated validity maintenance or extension fee;

(b) The owner declares relinquishment of the industrial property rights;

(c) The owner no longer exists, or the owner of a certificate of registered mark is no longer engaged in business activities and does not have a lawful heir;

OWNERS OF INDUSTRIAL PROPERTY OBJECTS

1. The owner of an invention, industrial design or layout design means an organization or individual who is granted a protection title for the respective industrial property object by the competent body.

Owner of a mark means an organization or individual who is granted a protection title for such mark by the competent body or who has an internationally registered mark recognized by the competent body or who has a well-known mark.

2. Owner of a trade name means an organization or individual who lawfully uses such trade name in business activities.

3. Owner of a trade secret means an organization or individual who has lawfully acquired such trade secret and kept it secret. A trade secret acquired by an employee or a performer of an assigned task during the performance of the hired job or assigned task shall be owned by the employer or the task assignor, unless otherwise agreed by the parties.

AUTHORS OF INVENTIONS, INDUSTRIAL DESIGNS AND LAYOUT DESIGNS AND THEIR RIGHTS

1. The author of an invention, industrial design or layout design means the person who has personally created such industrial property object. Where two or more persons have jointly created an industrial property object, they shall be co-authors of it.

2. Moral rights of authors of inventions, industrial designs and layout designs shall include the following rights:

(a) To be named as authors in invention patents, utility solution patents, industrial design patents or certificates of registered design of semi-conducting closed circuits;

(b) To be acknowledged as authors in documents in which inventions, industrial designs or layout designs are published or introduced.

3. Economic rights of authors of inventions, industrial designs and layout designs are the rights to receive remuneration.

ACTS OF INFRINGEMENT OF RIGHTS TO INVENTIONS, INDUSTRIAL DESIGNS AND LAYOUT DESIGNS

The following acts shall be regarded as infringements of rights of owners of inventions, industrial designs and layout designs:

1. Using protected inventions, protected industrial designs or industrial designs insignificantly different from protected industrial designs, or protected layout designs or any original part thereof within the valid term of a protection title without permission from the owners.

2. Using inventions, industrial designs and layout designs without paying compensation according to the provisions of Law on intellectual property.

ACTS OF INFRINGEMENT OF THE RIGHT TO TRADE SECRETS

The following acts shall be deemed infringements of the right to trade secrets:

(a) Accessing or acquiring information pertaining to a trade secret by taking acts against secrecy- keeping measures applied by lawful controllers of such trade secret;

(b) Disclosing or using information pertaining to a trade secret without the permission of the owner of such trade secret;

(c) Breaching secrecy-keeping contracts or deceiving, inducing, buying off, forcing, seducing or abusing the trust of persons in charge of secrecy-keeping in order to access, acquire or disclose a trade secret;

(d) Accessing or acquiring information pertaining to the trade secret of an applicant for a licence for trading in or circulating products by taking acts against secrecy-keeping measures applied by competent bodies;

ACTS OF INFRINGEMENT OF RIGHTS TO MARKS, TRADE NAMES AND GEOGRAPHICAL INDICATIONS

1. The following acts, if performed without the permission of mark owners, shall be deemed to be infringements of the right to a mark:

(a) Using signs identical with protected marks for goods or services identical with goods or services on the list registered together with such mark;

(b) Using signs identical with protected marks for goods or services similar or related to those goods or services on the list registered together with such mark, if such use is likely to cause confusion as to the origin of the goods or services;

(c) Using signs similar to protected marks for goods or services identical with, similar to or related to goods or services on the list registered together with such mark, if such use is likely to cause confusion as to the origin of the goods or services;

(d) Using signs identical with, or similar to, well known marks, or signs in the form of translations or transcriptions of well-known marks for any goods or services, including those not identical with, dissimilar or unrelated to goods or services on the lists of those bearing well known marks, if such use is likely to cause confusion as to the origin of the goods or services or misleading impressions as to the relationship between users of such signs and well known mark owners.

2. All acts of using commercial indications identical with, or similar to, trade names of others which were used earlier for the same or similar type of goods or services, which cause confusion as to business entities, establishments or activities under such trade names shall be deemed to be infringements of the right to the trade name.

3. The following acts shall be deemed to be infringements of the right to protected geographical indications:

(a) Using protected geographical indications for products which do not satisfy the criteria of peculiar characteristics and quality of products bearing geographical indications, although such products originate from geographical areas bearing such geographical indication;

(b) Using protected geographical indications for products similar to products bearing geographical indications for the purpose of taking advantage of their reputation and popularity;

(c) Using any sign identical with, or similar to, a protected geographical indication for products not originating from geographical areas bearing such geographical indication, and therefore misleading consumers into believing such products originate from such geographical areas;

(d) Using protected geographical indications of wines or spirits for wines or spirits not originating from geographical areas bearing such geographical indication, even where the true origin of goods is indicated or geographical indications are used in the form of translations or transcriptions, or accompanied by such words as "category," "model," "type," "imitation" or the like.

ACTS OF UNFAIR COMPETITION

The following acts shall be deemed to be acts of unfair competition:

(a) Using commercial indications to cause confusion as to business entities, business activities or commercial origin of goods or services;

(b) Using commercial indications to cause confusion as to the origin, production method, utilities, quality, quantity or other characteristics of goods or services; or as to the conditions for provision of goods or services;

(c) Registering or possessing the right to use or using domain names identical with, or confusingly similar to, protected trade names or marks of others, or geographical indications without having the right to use, for the purpose of possessing such domain name, benefiting from or prejudicing the reputation and popularity of the respective mark, trade name or geographical indication.

OBLIGATION TO USE INVENTIONS AND MARKS

1. Owners of inventions shall be obliged to manufacture protected products or apply protected processes to satisfy the requirements of national defence and security, disease prevention, and treatment and nutrition of the people or to meet other social urgent needs.

2. Owners of marks shall be obliged to use such marks continuously. Where a mark has not been used for five consecutive years or more, the ownership right to such mark shall be invalidated in accordance with the provisions of Law on intellectual property.

GENERAL PROVISIONS ON ASSIGNMENT OF INDUSTRIAL PROPERTY RIGHTS

1. Assignment of an industrial property right means the transfer of ownership right by the owner of such industrial property right to another organization or individual.

2. An assignment of an industrial property right must be established in the form of a written contract (hereinafter referred to as an industrial property right assignment contract).

RESTRICTIONS ON ASSIGNMENT OF INDUSTRIAL PROPERTY RIGHTS

1. Industrial property right owners may only assign their rights within the scope of protection.

2. Rights to geographical indications shall not be assignable.

3. Rights to trade names may only be assigned together with the transfer of the entire business establishment and business activities under such trade name.

4. The assignment of the rights to marks must not cause confusion as to properties or origins of goods or services bearing such marks.

5. Rights to marks may only be assigned to organizations or individuals who satisfy conditions for persons having the right to register such marks.

CONTENTS OF INDUSTRIAL PROPERTY RIGHT ASSIGNMENT CONTRACTS

An industrial property right assignment contract must contain the following principal contents:

1. Full names and addresses of the assignor and of the assignee.
2. Grounds for the assignment.
3. Assignment price.
4. Rights and obligations of the assignor and the assignee.

LICENSING OF INDUSTRIAL PROPERTY RIGHTS

1. Licensing of an industrial property object means permission by the owner of such industrial property object for another organization or individual to use the industrial property object within the scope of the owner's right.

2. Licensing of industrial property objects must be established in the form of a written contract (hereinafter referred to as industrial property object licence contract).

RESTRICTIONS ON LICENSING OF INDUSTRIAL PROPERTY OBJECTS

1. The right to use geographical indications or trade names shall not be licensable.

2. The right to use collective marks must not be licensed to organizations or individuals other than members of the owners of such collective marks.

3. The licensee must not enter into a sub-licence contract with a third party, unless it is so permitted by the licensor.

4. Mark licensees shall be obliged to indicate on goods and goods packages that such goods have been manufactured under mark licence contracts.

5. Invention licensees under exclusive contracts shall be obliged to use such inventions in the same manner as the invention owners according to the provisions of Law on intellectual property.

TYPES OF INDUSTRIAL PROPERTY OBJECT LICENCE CONTRACTS

Industrial property object licence contracts shall be of the following types:

1. Exclusive contract means a contract under which, within the licensing scope and term, the licensee shall have the exclusive right to use the licensed industrial property object while the licensor may neither enter into any industrial property object licence contract with any third party nor, without permission from the licensee, use such industrial property object.

2. Non-exclusive contract means a contract under which, within the licensing scope and term, the licensor shall still have the right to use the industrial property object and to enter into a non-exclusive industrial property object licence contract with others.

3. Industrial property object sub-licence contract means a contract under which the licensor is a licensee of the right to use such industrial property object pursuant to another contract.

CONTENTS OF INDUSTRIAL PROPERTY OBJECT LICENCE CONTRACTS

1. An industrial property object licence contract must contain the following principal contents:

(a) Full names and addresses of the licensor and of the licensee;

(b) Grounds for licensing;

(c) Contract type;

(d) Licensing scope including limitations on use right and territorial limitations;

(dd) Contract term;

(e) Licensing price;

(g) Rights and obligations of the licensor and of the licensee.

2. An industrial property object licence contract must not have provisions which unreasonably restrict the right of the licensee, and in particular the following provisions which do not derive from the rights

of the licensor:

(a) Prohibiting the licensee from improving the industrial property object other than marks; compelling the licensee to transfer free of charge to the licensor improvements of the industrial property object made by the licensee or the right of industrial property registration or industrial property rights to such improvements;

(b) Directly or indirectly restricting the licensee from exporting goods produced or services provided under the industrial property object licence contract to the territories where the licensor neither holds the respective industrial property right nor has the exclusive right to import such goods;

(c) Compelling the licensee to buy all or a certain percentage of raw materials, components or equipment from the licensor or a third party designated by the licensor not for the purpose of ensuring the quality of goods produced or services provided by the licensee;

(d) Prohibiting the licensee from complaining about or initiating lawsuits with regard to the validity of the industrial property rights or the licensor's right to license.

INDUSTRIAL PROPERTY REPRESENTATION SERVICES

1. Industrial property representation services shall comprise:

(a) Representing organizations or individuals before competent State bodes in the establishment and enforcement of industrial property rights;

(b) Providing consultancy on issues related to procedures for the establishment and enforcement of industrial property rights;

(c) Other services related to procedures for the establishment and enforcement of industrial property rights.

2. Industrial property representatives shall comprise organizations providing industrial property representation services (hereinafter referred to as industrial property representation service organizations) and individuals practicing industrial property representation within such organizations (hereinafter referred to as industrial property agents).

SCOPE OF RIGHTS OF INDUSTRIAL PROPERTY REPRESENTATIVES

1. Industrial property representation service organizations shall only provide services within the scope of authorization and may re-authorize other industrial property representation service organizations when they obtain written consent from the authorizing parties.

2. Industrial property representation service organizations may voluntarily waive their industrial property representation service business after having lawfully transferred all incomplete representation jobs to other industrial property representation service organizations.

3. Industrial property representatives must not perform the following activities:

(a) Concurrently represent different parties in dispute over industrial property rights;

(b) Withdraw applications for protection titles, declare waiver of protection or withdraw appeals against the establishment of industrial property rights without consent from the authorizing parties;

(c) Deceive their clients regarding contracts for industrial property representation services or force their clients to enter into and perform such contracts.

RESPONSIBILITIES OF INDUSTRIAL PROPERTY REPRESENTATIVES

1. Industrial property representatives shall have the following responsibilities:

(a) To clearly notify fee and charge amounts and rates related to procedures for establishment and enforcement of industrial property rights, and service charge amounts and rates according to the service charge tariff registered at the State administrative body for industrial property rights;

(b) To keep confidential information and documents related to cases in which they act as representatives;

(c) To truthfully and fully inform represented parties of all notices and requests from the State body competent to establish and enforce industrial property rights; to deliver on time to the represented parties protection titles and other decisions;

(d) To protect the rights and legitimate interests of represented parties by promptly satisfying all requests regarding represented parties from the State body competent to establish and enforce industrial property rights;

(dd) To notify the State body competent to establish and enforce industrial property rights of all changes in the names, addresses of and other information about the represented parties when necessary.

2. Industrial property representation service organizations shall be civilly liable to the represented parties for representation performed by industrial property agents on behalf of such service organizations.

CONDITIONS APPLICABLE TO INDUSTRIAL PROPERTY REPRESENTATION SERVICE BUSINESS

Organizations which satisfy the following conditions shall be permitted to provide industrial property representation services as industrial property representation service organizations:

1. Being a business or organization which practises law, or a scientific and technological service organization lawfully established and operating.

2. Having the function of providing industrial property representation services, which is stated in its business registration certificate or operation registration certificate (hereinafter both referred to as business registration certificate).

3. The head of such organization or person authorized by the head must satisfy the conditions for industrial property representation service practice stipulated in clause 1 of article 155 of Law on intellectual property.

CONDITIONS APPLICABLE TO INDUSTRIAL PROPERTY REPRESENTATION SERVICE PRACTICES

An individual who satisfies the following conditions shall be permitted to practice industrial property representation service:

(a) Having an industrial property representation service practising certificate;

(b) Working for one industrial property representation service organization.

ORGANIZATIONS AND INDIVIDUALS WHOSE RIGHTS TO PLANT VARIETIES ARE ELIGIBLE FOR PROTECTION

Organizations and individuals whose rights to plant varieties are eligible for protection means those who select and breed or discover and develop plant varieties or who invest in the selection and breeding or the discovery and development of plant varieties or to whom rights to plant varieties are transferred.

DISTINCTNESS OF A PLANT VARIETY

A plant variety shall be deemed to be distinct if it is clearly distinguishable from any other variety whose existence is a matter of common knowledge at the time of filing the application or on the priority date, as the case may be.

UNIFORMITY OF A PLANT VARIETY

A plant variety shall be deemed uniform if, subject to variation which may be expected from the particular features of its propagation, it is sufficiently uniform in its relevant characteristics.

STABILITY OF A PLANT VARIETY

A plant variety shall be deemed stable if its relevant originally described characteristics remain unchanged after repeated propagation or, in the case of a particular cycle of propagation, at the end of each cycle.

LICENSING OF PLANT VARIETIES

1. Licensing of a plant variety means permission from the protection certificate holder to another person to conduct one or more acts within the holder's right to use the plant variety.

2. Where the right to use a plant variety is under co-ownership, the licensing of such plant variety to another person must be consented to by all co-owners.

3. The licensing of a plant variety must be affected in the form of a written contract.

4. A plant variety licensing contract must not contain terms which unreasonably restrict the rights of the licensee, particularly restrictions neither deriving from nor aimed at protecting the rights of the licensor to the licensed plant variety.

RIGHTS OF PARTIES TO A LICENSING CONTRACT

1. The licensor shall have the right to permit or not permit the licensee to sub-license to a third party.

2. The licensee shall have the following rights:

(a) To license the use right to a third party if so, permitted by the licensor;

(b) To request the licensor to take necessary and appropriate measures to prevent infringement by a third-party causing loss and damage to the licensee;

ASSIGNMENT OF RIGHTS TO PLANT VARIETIES

1. Assignment of rights to a plant variety means the transfer by the plant variety protection certificate holder to the assignee of all rights to such plant variety. The assignee shall become the plant variety protection certificate holder from the date of registration of the assignment contract with the State administrative body for rights to plant varieties in accordance with procedures stipulated by law.

2. Where rights to a plant variety are under joint ownership, the assignment of such rights to another person must be consented to by all co-owners.

3. The assignment of rights to a plant variety must be affected in the form of written contract.

RIGHT TO SELF-PROTECTION

1. An intellectual property right holder shall have the right to apply the following measures to protect the intellectual property rights of such holder:

(a) To apply technological measures to prevent acts of infringement of its intellectual property rights;

(b) To request any organization or individual who commits an act of infringement of the intellectual property rights of the holder to terminate such act, make a public apology or rectification, and pay damages;

(c) To request the competent State body to deal with acts of infringement of its intellectual property rights in accordance with the provisions of Law on intellectual property and other relevant laws;

(d) To initiate a lawsuit at a court or a claim at an arbitration centre to protect the legitimate rights and interests of the holder.

2. Organizations and individuals who suffer loss and damage caused by acts of infringement of intellectual property rights or who discover acts of infringement of intellectual property rights which cause loss and damage to consumers or society shall have the right to request the competent State body to deal with such acts in accordance with the provisions of Law on intellectual property and other relevant laws.

REMEDIES WHEN DEALING WITH ACTS OF INFRINGEMENT OF INTELLECTUAL PROPERTY RIGHTS

1. Any organization or individual who commits an act of infringement of the intellectual property rights of another organization or individual shall, depending upon the nature and seriousness of such infringement, be dealt with by the application of civil, administrative or criminal remedies.

2. In necessary cases, the competent State body may apply provisional urgent measures, measures to control intellectual property related imports and exports, preventive measures and measures to secure enforcement of an administrative penalty in accordance with the provisions of Law on intellectual property and other relevant laws.

AUTHORITY FOR DEALING WITH ACTS OF INFRINGEMENT OF INTELLECTUAL PROPERTY RIGHTS

1. The following bodies shall, within the scope of their respective duties and powers, have authority to deal with acts of infringement of intellectual property rights: courts, inspectorates, market management offices, customs offices, police offices and people's committees at all levels.

2. The application of civil and criminal remedies shall fall within the authority of courts. In necessary cases, courts may apply provisional urgent measures stipulated by law.

3. The application of administrative remedies shall fall within the authority of inspectorates, police offices, market management offices, customs offices and people's committees at all levels. In necessary cases, such bodies may apply preventive measures stipulated by law or measures to secure payment of administrative fines stipulated by law.

4. The application of measures to control intellectual property related imports and exports shall fall within the authority of customs offices.

CIVIL REMEDIES

Courts may apply the following civil remedies in dealing with organizations and individuals who have committed acts of infringement of intellectual property rights:

1. Compulsory termination of the infringing acts.

2. Compulsory public apology and rectification.

3. Compulsory performance of civil obligations.

4. Compulsory payment of damages for loss.

5. Compulsory destruction, distribution or use for non-commercial purposes of goods, raw materials and materials, and facilities used principally for the production or trading of goods which infringed intellectual property rights, provided that such destruction, distribution or use will not affect the exploitation of rights by intellectual property right holders.

PRINCIPLES FOR DETERMINING LOSS AND DAMAGE CAUSED BY AN INFRINGEMENT OF INTELLECTUAL PROPERTY RIGHTS

1. Loss and damage caused by acts of infringement of industrial property rights shall comprise:

(a) Material loss and damage including property loss, decrease in income and profit, loss of business opportunity, and reasonable expenses for mitigating and remedying the material damage;

(b) Spiritual loss and damage including damage to honour, dignity, prestige, reputation and other spiritual loss caused to authors of literary, artistic and scientific works; to performers; to authors of inventions, industrial designs, layout designs; and to breeders of plant varieties.

2. The extent of damage shall be determined on the basis of actual losses suffered by intellectual property right holders due to acts of infringement of intellectual property rights.

Conclusion

Thank you again for downloading this book on *"LAW ON INTELLECTUAL PROPERTY: Essential Legal Terms Explained You Need To Know About Trademarks, Copyrights, Patents, and Trade Secrets""* and reading all the way to the end. I'm extremely grateful.

If you know of anyone else who may benefit from the informative legal words presented in this book, please help me inform them of this book. I would greatly appreciate it.

Finally, if you enjoyed this book and feel that it has added value to your study or career in any way, please take a couple of minutes to share your thoughts and post a REVIEW on Amazon. Your feedback will help me to continue to write the kind of Kindle books that helps you get results. Furthermore, if you write a simple REVIEW with positive words for this book on Amazon, you can help hundreds or perhaps thousands of other readers who may want to enhance their legal vocabulary have a chance getting what they need. Like you, they worked hard for every penny they spend on books. With the information and recommendation you provide, they would be more likely to take action right away. We really look forward to reading your review.

Thanks again for your support and good luck!

If you enjoy my book, please write a POSITIVE REVIEW on amazon.

-- Dr. Peter Johnson --

Check Out Other Books

Go here to check out other related books that might interest you:

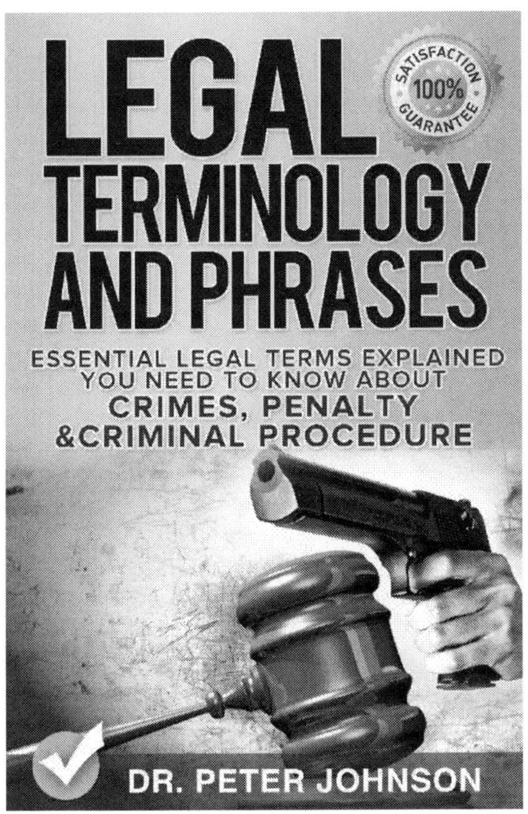

Legal Terminology And Phrases: Essential Legal Terms Explained You Need To Know About Crimes, Penalty And Criminal Procedure

http://www.amazon.com/dp/B01L5EB54Y

COMPANY LAW: Mastering Essential Legal Terms Explained About Limited Liability Companies, Joint-Stock Companies, Partnership, Private Enterprises, And Groups of Companies!

https://www.amazon.com/dp/B07P2PRVMJ

INVESTMENT LAW: Essential Legal Terms Explained You Need To Know About Law On Investment!

https://www.amazon.com/dp/B07P79D925

LABOR LAW: Essential Legal Terms Explained You Need To Know About Law On Labor!

https://www.amazon.com/dp/B07PFD2CML

CIVIL LAW: Mastering Essential Legal Terms Explained About Civil Rights, Guardianship, Civil Transactions, Civil Obligations, Civil Liability, Civil Contracts And Civil Procedure!

https://www.amazon.com/dp/B07P5GS8LD

Legal Vocabulary In Use: Master 600+ Essential Legal Terms And Phrases Explained In 10 Minutes A Day

http://www.amazon.com/dp/B01L0FKXPU

Civil Law Vocabulary In Use: Master 350+ Essential Civil Law Terms And Phrases Explained With Examples In 10 Minutes A Day.

https://www.amazon.com/dp/B0781TQWGV

Criminal Law Vocabulary In Use: Master 400+ Essential Criminal Law Terms And Phrases Explained With Examples In 10 Minutes A Day.

https://www.amazon.com/dp/B078KLR51Z

Administrative And Tax Law In Use : Master 300+ Administrative And Tax Law Terms And Phrases Explained With Examples In 10 Minutes A Day.

https://www.amazon.com/dp/B07JMD546J

Productivity Secrets For Students: The Ultimate Guide To Improve Your Mental Concentration, Kill Procrastination, Boost Memory And Maximize Productivity In Study

http://www.amazon.com/dp/B01JS52UT6

Shortcut To Ielts Writing: The Ultimate Guide To Immediately Increase Your Ielts Writing Scores

http://www.amazon.com/dp/B01JV7EQGG

44358784R00059

Made in the USA
Middletown, DE
06 May 2019